Close in Saltmarket, 1887.

AULD HAWKIE

and other
Glasgow
Characters

drawn by
Dorothy Whitaker

poems by Freddie Anderson, text by Joe Fisher

Glasgow District Libraries 1988

This book is dedicated to my father, Robert Johnston, who gifted me his love of Glasgow.

I would like to express my thanks to Bob McFarlane, Joe Fisher and Freddie Anderson, for their great assistance.

Illustrations © Dorothy Whitaker, 1988.
Poems © Freddie Anderson, 1988.
Text © Joe Fisher, 1988.
ISBN 0-906169-24-0.

Published by Glasgow District Libraries,
The Mitchell Library, North Street, Glasgow G3 7DN.

Typeset, originated and printed by
Holmes McDougall Printing, Glasgow & Edinburgh.

CONTENTS

FOREWORD

Society has always had to deal as it thought best with those poor unfortunates whose physical or mental disabilities rendered them incapable of earning a living by ordinary means. In Glasgow's eighteenth and early nineteenth centuries it was the task of the Church and the Town's Hospital to provide a bare modicum of relief for these anonymous figures, "the poor indigent children, the old decayed men and women, and others rendered unable to provide for themselves".

A few of them, a very few, however, refused to become anonymous, refused to relinquish their individualities — and in doing so earned themselves the sobriquet of "Characters". The names and careers of about twenty of them have come down to us, these defiant nonconformists with whom even Bailies and grand city magnates were not ashamed to indulge in verbal sword-play and whose sayings and actions amused and still amuse the citizens of Glasgow.

It is an ironic commentary on the whirligig of time that it is the once great men who are now completely forgotten, while the beggars, ballad singers and chapmen live on.

Fifteen of the most famous of these Glasgow characters have been selected and reinterpreted by Dorothy Whitaker in coloured versions of the original steel engravings. Freddie Anderson, Glasgow's folk-song practitioner, has fittingly embellished the booklet with his verses, and short notes have been provided by Joe Fisher, Librarian in charge of The Mitchell Library's Glasgow Collection.

1 : BLIND ALICK

Some poets they come from Parnassus,
And some from the side of the road,
But the "Fiddler's Close" in the High Street
Was the Homer of Glasgow's abode.

He scraped out his tunes by the Trongait
And powerful poems for narration,
T'is said that Blind Alick of Glasgow
Was McGonagle's first inspiration.

The best known of all these characters was Blind Alick (Alexander Macdonald). Born in 1771 in the north of England he was rendered blind by childhood smallpox. However he had an excellent ear for the fiddle, and it was this talent which provided him with a living when he settled in Glasgow in 1790. He was regularly engaged to play at penny reels and weddings — 1/6d for the first two hours, then 1d for each reel after that. A blind poet, he was often called the Glasgow Homer, and celebrated his country's victories in verse which anticipated many of the felicities of the great McGonagle. Here is his account of a famous naval victory:—

"We have gained a mighty fight
On the sea at Camperdown,
Our cannon they did rattle, lads
And we knocked their topmasts down;
But the particulars you will hear
By the post in the afternoon."

His love of the life of the city streets was only surpassed by his love of *aqua vitae,* for he would sooner take his reward in the shape of a dram than as two bawbees. Despite his hard life and hard drinking he lived to the ripe old age (for these days) of fifty-nine, dying peacefully in a hospital bed.

2 : HIRSTLIN' KATE

See Hirstlin' Kate o' the town
On her brushes go sweepin' round,
Some heads may be high
Peerin' into the sky,
But Katie's is fixed on the ground,

The bawbees she spies there below,
And buttons an' pins in a row,
So close to the earth
Gives her senses more worth,
She can hear the very grass grow.

About 1812 this poor unfortunate creature could be seen creeping about the Glasgow streets between the Calton Mouth in the east and Jamaica Street in the west. Having lost nearly all use of her legs she "hirstled" along on a little low cart in a most peculiar manner. In one hand she held an old bauchle [shoe]; her good foot was shod with its partner, and by the dexterous use of these two limbs she propelled herself through the city streets. Her appearance was coarse, masculine and haggard and her tattered and bedraggled skirts constantly swept the city's dirty cobblestones, yet this extremely unprepossessing figure was eagerly sought after by the children. The breast of her ragged dress was stuck all over with pins, and for each one given to her she would sing in a cracked voice for her child audiences verse after verse of the old songs and ballads.

3 : AULD HAWKIE

O gather round till I tell you my tale
O' the times I was jovial an' hearty an' hale,
But this prick-the-louse tailor's attention was such
That I limp 'round the town on this tattered auld crutch.

At Glasgow Cross fairings or doon by the Green,
That's where the bold Hawkie's aye tae be seen,
Wi' hundreds around him an' mony a fool
Come to learn what he should have been taught at the School.

They ask me conundrums about this, about that,
What are the stars, an' who belled the cat?
The craziest questions an' that sort o' kind
Would drive a Feelosopher out of his mind.

But they can't stump Auld Hawkie, not one little bit,
To answer their riddles I'm able an' fit;
If ye want, come an' try me, I'm aye to be seen
Doon by Airn's Well at the foot o' the Green.

William Cameron was left with a crooked right leg following a boyhood accident while apprenticed to a tailor. He travelled through Scotland and the north of England as a hedge-preacher, strolling actor, toy-maker and china mender. He took to begging, then settled down in Glasgow in 1818 as a ballad seller. One of his successes was a chapbook called "The Prophecies of Hawkie, a Cow" from which he took his nickname. Although his wares may have been ordinary, his eloquence was not. Peter Mackenzie describes him as "one of the greatest and wittiest beggars that ever infested the streets of Glasgow". He died in 1851, but his "autobiography" was published in 1888, a curious work which provides an excellent insight into the world of the beggars.

4 : JAMIE BLUE

A sage of the streets,
He knew every sang
To the grandeur o' Scotia
Will ever belang!
Tannahill was his friend
And Burns was his seer,
His wealth was his wit,
He had no earthly gear!
Slagging Auld Hawkie
Was part of his play,
Each livened the city
In his own different way!
Though in old Govan Poor-house
He died in poverty,
His fame extends to years beyond
The reach of royalty.

Jamie Blue's proper name was James McIndoe, an old soldier who had been drummed out of the 71st Regiment. He was described as a "dealer in hardware, leeches, spurious pepper and blue" and was also well known as a ballad singer and speech crier. His odd nicknames "Jamie Blue" and "Blue Thumbs" he earned because of the colour of his hands from his trade in indigo-coloured buttons. He was an inveterate enemy and rival of Hawkie and strenuously maintained that he had stolen Jamie's position as Glasgow's "Head Speech Crier". He died in 1837.

5 : BELL GEORDIE

Bell Geordie, Bell Geordie
Dressed like a lordy,
Parading the causey of Tron,
Proclaiming the news,
The Council's grand views
And lamenting poor souls who were gone.

Bell Geordie, Bell Geordie,
Lived like a lordy,
Well, hardly, an' that isn't fair,
But he won't ring his bell
For his departed sel',
He'll only in spirit be there.

The bellman was an important person in the days when the local newspaper carried no local news. He perambulated the city thoroughfares, attracting the lieges' attention by ringing his bell then making his official announcements in "a clear and audible voice". At one time he might be forthtelling that James Hodge's wife's niece dressed dead corpses, at another that Mrs Lamont in the Stockwell Entry had soups ready everyday from 12 to 2. The best known of these criers was undoubtedly George Gibson, alias Bell Geordie. As he walked through the city in the 1790's in his red livery coat, its gilt buttons decorated with the city arms, and his blue plush breeches, white stockings, buckled shoes and cocked hat, he was famous for his ability to announce his often pedestrian news in rough rhymes and for his caustic humour. The latter brought about his downfall for he claimed that the Bailies were as much the town's servants as himself. Instantly dismissed, he ended his days, silent and stone blind, being led through the streets by a little girl, thankful for the smallest pittance.

Fiddler's Close, 1830.

Dorothy Whitaker 1987

Bridgegate Street, 1828.

6 : THE REVEREND JOHN AITKEN

The most unique o' clergymen
Who ever graced the Green,
That open-air cathedral
Upon the Glasgow scene.
A man of truth and learning
In every word he spoke;
He popularised the Bible
With many a hearty joke.
No glum or gloomy preacher
He lived among the poor,
Redeeming by his human touch
Many an evil-doer.
Scores of his disciples
Followed him with pride,
The imprints of the stable-born
Upon the Banks o' Clyde.

The Reverend John Aitken was a self-ordained "minister" who came of Calton weaving stock. He had in his youth received a good education and used the remnants of it to deliver public "preachments", generally at the entrance to Glasgow Green from the Saltmarket. His style of pulpit oratory was celebrated in a contemporary stanza:—

"Stop here, an' pitch a bawbee in my Plate.
I'll gie ye Gospel for't, the best I can.
I'm puir, unbeneficed an' cauld's my Pate,
My Kirk is space, my Hearers, anyman."

His equipment was extremely simple — a three-legged stool, a pewter plate and an old fir chair — and his sermons strong meat, full of fire and brimstone.

7 : THE MAJOR AND MARY

A Solemn Dirge

Frae the Gushet to the Calton Cross,
Let naught but grief your minds engross,
The city has sustained a loss,
*   Past a' remeid:*
For, 'mang the grave-yard's clammy dross,
*   Lies Major deid.*

Nae mair will he wi' rattlin' birr,
Sing to his soul-inspiring' girr,
The dormant Gothamites to stir,
*   His powers to heed;*
For, snug he lies, enclosed wi' fir,
*   Cauld, stiff an' deid.*

It to my heart gies muckle pain,
Sic worth on paper thus to stain,
In life he was surpassed by nane.
*   Now a' tak heed!*
His like ye'll never see again,
*   Since Major's deid.*

But why omit his fond soul-mate,
His better hauf sae blythe an' blate,
For linked together was their fate,
*   Like word an' deed,*
As Major went, he held the gate,
*   An' baith are deid.*

Sandy Rogers (1832) and Freddie Anderson

The poor Major's claim to fame was his appearance and his behaviour. Peter Mackenzie, in his *Old Reminiscences of Glasgow*, described him as "round-shouldered, twisted, knock-kneed, splae-footed, his head projecting from the nape of his neck like a duck choking on a rebellious potato". The Major sang over and over some doggerel lines while he "accompanied" himself on two sticks, capering about in the queerest of contortions. Here again Peter Mackenzie has a telling phrase — "a fair representation of an isoceles triangle gone mad". The dance was actually a *pas de deux*. His partner was Coal Mary, so called from her earlier employment — carrying sacks of coal up the stairs of the Glasgow tenements. This gentle soul was captivated by the Major and joined in his crazy cavortings. Apart from a penchant for dressing in blue and for carrying scraps of food about her person in many little pokes, history has nothing more to say about her. Major and Mary were swept away within 48 hours of each other in the cholera outbreak of 1832.

8 : RAB HA'

Rab Ha's Snack Luncheon

Eight stone o' tatties,
A basket full o' fish,
A basin crammed wi' butter beans
Just starts his little dish:
Thirteen head o' cabbage,
A cauldron choked wi' sauce,
A barrow-load o' turnips
And Carrigeen moss,
Five stone o' carrots,
Wi' sausages fried broon,
And three Kelvin ponds o' whisky
Tae wash the wee snack doon.

Robert Hall was celebrated in his day throughout all the west of Scotland as Rab Ha', the Glesca Glutton. He had been a farm labourer but had early abandoned settled employment for the life of a vagrant, and was a constant attender at all the horse races, fox hunts and coursing in the district. So great was his appetite that no one who wagered on his gastronomic powers on such occasions was likely to lose his bet. It is recorded that only once was he beaten, and that by a most curious dish — a saucerful of oysters mixed with cream and ground lump sugar! He died in a hayloft in Hutchesontown in 1843.

9 : PENNY-A-YARD

Come a' you fine matrons an' belles o' Clydeside,
Mak yoursel' braw for the ships on the tide,
A kiss an' a cuddle will be your reward,
Sae hoop up your skirts wi' a penny-a-yard.

Their eyes they will shine as the lads disembark,
An' lovers'll stroll thro' sweet Kelvin Park,
Frae the glaur an' the dust your gear ye can guard, –
Jist buy as ye need frae auld "Penny-a-Yard".

Amongst the many ballad singers, blind fiddlers and vendors of small wares who frequented the Saltmarket, none was stranger than Edward Finlay, wire-worker, born about 1800. Over one shoulder he slung a coil of shining wire from which, with the aid of a small pair of pliers, he skilfully created long lengths of chain which he draped, ready for sale, over his other shoulder. Strange to say, these chains of his met with a ready sale amongst the Glasgow housewives and small traders, and his sales-cry — "Penny-a-yard" — became the name by which he was known throughout the city. He also had a fair degree of ingenuity which he exercised by twisting his raw material into intricate wire-puzzles. As another sideline, he often concocted arithmetical puzzles which he printed and sold, demonstrating their solutions with the aid of chalk and a board.

Close, 75 High Street, 1880.

Castle Street and Cathedral Tower, 18th century.

10 : WEE JAMIE WALLACE

I see his shadow in the market place,
Where later Matt McGinn was born to sing the Calton
Of our day, and in his way
He was the same lone figure watching the stalls,
The fruit and sandwiches, often quite hungrily.
A small almost dwarf-like man stunted in growth
Like so many Glasgow's poor, victim of the greedy evil doer.
Kindly shone his sun occasionally; when low, depressed and ill
A rich friend took him to his house outside the city,
And pity replaced with green fields the ricketty, straw-roofed, vile dens
The dark satanic mills, the barras' decaying fruit smells,
Booze from the "Sarry Heid" of Gallowgate.
Wee Jamie saw clear skies and lost for a time all jealousy and hate.
And then after a month, back to his post poorly paid,
Watching the fruit and stalls, carrying baskets.
I see him like a faint figure, but clearly,
As on Keats' eternal urn,
A symbolical sentinel by-passed in history except for Mackenzie's pen, a sympathetic artist,
And this book, like most are by-passed though their day will dawn.

Wee Jamie Wallace caught the city's fancy and became elevated to the rank of a "character". His chief claim to fame was his post as self-appointed "officer" in the Scotch Fruit Market in Kent Street. Occasionally he would retire for a while from his duties; two versions exist of where he went. One is poetically set out above; the other was that he went to the Parliamentary Road Poorhouse! Then he would return to take up his superintendence of the gooseberries, plums, pears and apples from the
Clydeside orchards.

11 : WEE WILLIE WHITE

Ode

Poor blind endearing warbler of these streets
Which flow by ancient Clutha's tireless streams
And in an age when wealth accumulates
Beyond the peak of Avarice's dreams,
And yet you came from some gray, sunless Close
Or from the shadows of a wretched Wynd,
And for a meagre pittance to survive,
You played upon the heartstrings of mankind.
Oh, when great sails have found their last horizon
And once proud names are merely writ in sand,
The timeless tunes of your sweet magic flute
Shall echo o'er the bright resurgent land.

William White was a blind street musician. In physique he was broad and stout, standing scarcely five feet high. He patrolled the Trongate from the Steeple to Jamaica Street playing patriotic and popular songs on his tin whistle. He was a great favourite with everyone and many of the city notables would salute him as they passed. The sums he earned by his musical talents enabled him to live in what a contemporary account described as "respectable poverty". He died in 1858 and, a reflection on the *mores* of the society of the time, his admirers purchased a lair for him in the Southern Necropolis and decorated it with a carved representation of his tin whistle and the box he carried it in.

12 : BIG RACHEL

"Big Rachel o' Partick's an ogre",
Sae cried the lads o' that pairt,
But she lifted them up at the collar
And bundled them into her cairt:
An' it's off tae Marine Polis Station
Where they'll cool their daft heels for the night.
For ye can't tak' a lend o' Big Rachel
That colossus in girth an' in height.

"Stop scabbing", cried oot the wee worker,
"Get back to your crinoline frock!".
But almost before he quite knew it,
He was low on the ground with the shock.
"Tak' that an' tak' that", as she biffed him,
"I ken that your name is O'Grady,
Ye wee dirty nyaff frae the Goosedubs –
How daur ye insult a fine lady!"

Yes, your Suffragettes soon'll be rising,
As Progress spreads over the Earth,
An' the Feminist Movement in glory
Just to-morrow is coming to birth!
Big Rachel forestalled all predictions
Such contempt for all men she has got,
"Men equal! ! !" she cried with a snigger,
"I'd murder the whole bloody lot!"

Mrs Rachel Hamilton, born in the north of Ireland in 1829, was an outstanding woman — over 6ft tall! She was by turn a labourer with Todd & McGregor, shipbuilders, a forewoman navvy at the Jordanhill Brickworks, and a farm worker on an Anniesland farm. During the Partick Riots in the early "Seventies" she acted as a special constable. She died in Dumbarton Road, Partick, in 1899, aged 70.

13 : OLD MALABAR

"One bawbee more, the ball goes up",
I heard the strange, loud shout.
I scratched my head in wonder there
At what it's all about.

Above the crowd this heavy ball
Did to the skies ascend –
And should it fall upon his head,
His very life will end.

Higher, higher, higher still,
This ball went up and up,
And when it fell he caught it in
A solid leather cup.

This cup was strapped around his brow,
On each side an old scar!
Drouth may drive some folk to drink,
But not old Malabar.

Old Malabar was unique amongst the Glasgow characters by being neither a beggar, nor an eccentric nor a ballad singer, but a street showman-entertainer. Dressed in his colourful Oriental robes and accompanied by his faithful wife who looked after his props, he was always able to attract a street crowd. He juggled, he swallowed swords, but his *tour de force* was when he hurled a heavy metal ball high into the air and caught it in a cup bound to his forehead. He seldom indulged in ardent spirits; once he did, and during his next performance he failed to catch the ball properly in the cup. The result was a scar which he carried to the day of his death at 80 years of age in 1888.

14 : THE CLINCHER

A braw auld man,
A dandy in his day,
The only Glasgow man wi' proof
His heid was not astray.

Sauchiehall Street was his pitch –
He often daundered there.
At times he took the longer route
Doon tae St Enoch Square.

He wrote an' sold his ain newssheet,
"The Clincher" it was called,
An' mony's the time afore the Court
The brave auld chap was hauled.

Some know their Royals, some their luck
An' some a load o' corn,
But if the Clincher ye did miss
Ye were nae Glesca-born!

The Clincher, alias Alexander Petrie, was a barber by trade, but first and foremost he was a character of the purest water. A kenspeckle figure in his immaculate top hat, he was notorious throughout the city for the tongue-lashings he freely distributed, either verbally or through the pages of his very own newspaper *"The Clincher"* and mainly directed at his constant enemies the Town Council and the Police Department. Taken to the local asylum, he was released with a certificate, and thereafter he boasted of being the only Glaswegian officially to be declared sane!

Alexander Petrie died peacefully in hospital in 1937. Blind Alick having been born in 1771, our fifteen "characters" thus span over a century and a half, during which time they brought pleasure to the citizens of Glasgow and cocked a snook at fate, officialdom and "poortith cauld"!